W9-AHJ-363

Ancient
Innovations

The Technology of
Ancient Greece

Kate Shoup

Cavendish
Square

New York

Published in 2017 by Cavendish Square Publishing, LLC
243 5th Avenue, Suite 136, New York, NY 10016

Library of Congress Cataloging-in-Publication Data

Names: Shoup, Kate, 1972- author.
Title: The technology of Ancient Greece / Kate Shoup.
Description: New York : Cavendish Square Publishing, [2017] |
Series: Ancient innovations | Includes bibliographical references and index.
Identifiers: LCCN 2016021841 | ISBN 9781502622310 (library bound) | ISBN 9781502622327 (ebook)
Subjects: LCSH: Technology--Greece--History--Juvenile literature. |
Science--Greece--History--Juvenile literature. |
Greece--Civilization--Juvenile literature. | Greece--History--To 146 B.C.--Juvenile literature.
Classification: LCC T16 .S47 2017 | DDC 609.38--dc23
LC record available at https://lccn.loc.gov/2016021841

Editorial Director: David McNamara
Editor: Kristen Susienka
Copy Editor: Nathan Heidelberger
Associate Art Director: Amy Greenan
Designer: Joseph Macri
Production Assistant: Karol Szymczuk
Photo Research: J8 Media

Contents

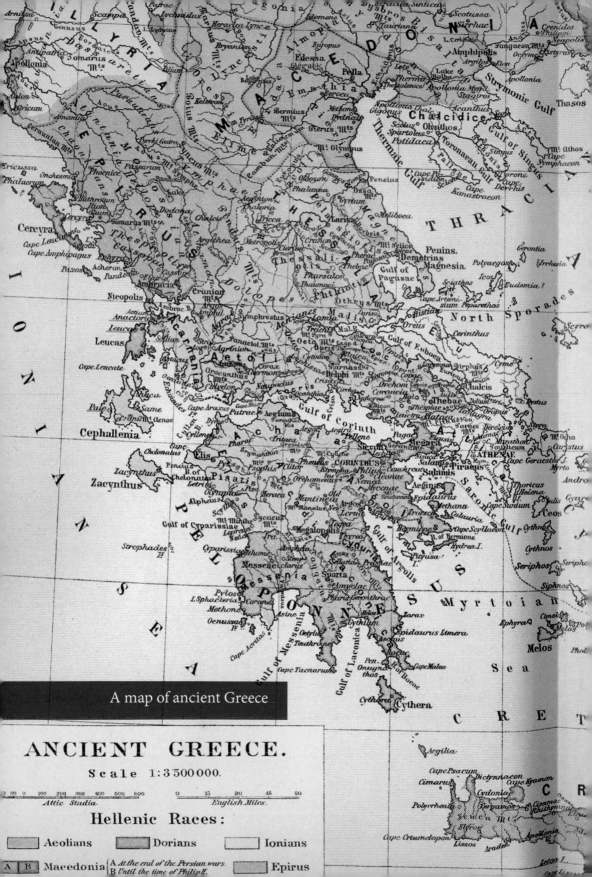

A map of ancient Greece

Chapter One

The History of Ancient Greece

Many people call ancient Greece, or *Hellas*, the "cradle of Western civilization." That's because the early Greeks made many advancements that became the foundation of Western thought and learning.

The Minoans and the Mycenaeans

In 1900, a British archaeologist named Arthur Evans discovered the remains of an ancient civilization on the island of Crete. Evans named this civilization the Minoan civilization, after King Minos. According to Greek myth, Minos was the first king of Crete. This Minoan civilization, considered the first ancient Greek society, arose around 3000 BCE.

Evidence shows that the Minoans were a peaceful people. They were more interested in trade than in warfare. An advanced society— historian Will Durant called it "the first link in the European chain"— the Minoans are known for their art. Several **frescoes** from this era have survived. So have many examples of Minoan pottery, which are often decorated with floral and marine themes. The Minoans were also among the first societies to develop a writing system. Historians call this system Linear A.

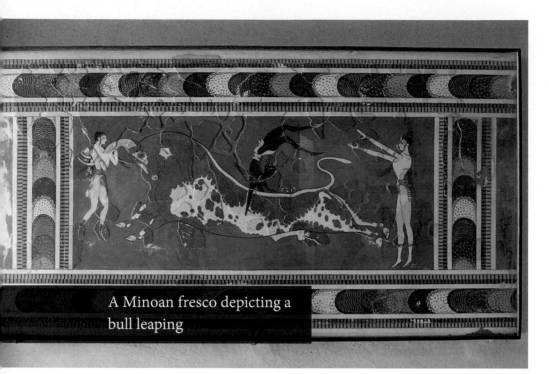

A Minoan fresco depicting a bull leaping

Around 1600 BCE, another civilization took root: the Mycenaean civilization. This society grew on the Peloponnesus, a large region separated from mainland Greece by the Gulf of Corinth. The Mycenaeans were the first to practice the **polytheistic** religion of ancient Greece. But unlike later Greeks, who believed Zeus was the supreme ruler, the Mycenaeans thought Poseidon was king of the gods. Like the Minoans, the Mycenaeans had a written language, now called Linear B. This language contained almost two hundred signs and symbols.

However, whereas the Minoans were peaceful, the Mycenaeans were warlike. They had a rigid, hierarchical society. Indeed, it's believed that a Mycenaean invasion brought down the Minoan civilization around 1400 BCE. (Some scholars claim a natural event, such as a volcanic eruption, was to blame.)

In 1100 BCE, the Mycenaeans, too, died out. Some believe this was at the hands of invaders. Others say it was the result of a natural disaster or even climate change.

The Archaic Period

After the fall of the Minoans and Mycenaeans, Greece entered a dark age. Of this period, few signs of culture remain. Finally, around 900 BCE, indications of a civilization resurface as written records begin to appear. Historians call this new period the archaic period.

During the archaic period, the population of ancient Greece grew more than tenfold, from eight hundred thousand to a whopping ten to thirteen million. To accommodate the growing population, the ancient Greeks built several colonies abroad. Eventually, these colonies spanned Asia Minor, Cyprus, Thrace, Ukraine, Russia, Illyria, Sicily, southern Italy, southern France, Corsica, Spain, Egypt, and Libya. By colonizing, the Greeks also created an extensive trading network.

Greeks of the archaic period organized themselves into several **city-states**. These included Athens, Argos, Smyrna, Corinth, and Sparta. A city-state is a city that is also a sovereign state. It has its own government and economy. Although each city-state was its own distinct entity, their inhabitants, who we now call the "ancient Greeks," shared a common language, religion, and culture.

The archaic period saw advancements in many aspects of ancient Greek culture—politics, philosophy, science, and the arts, including architecture, sculpture, and pottery. The earliest surviving examples of Greek poetry were composed during this era, using the new Greek alphabet. This new alphabet stemmed from the Phoenician alphabet. The Greek alphabet uses different letters from the English alphabet. Instead of letters like A, B, and C, the Greek alphabet uses symbols such as Δ (delta), Π (pi), and Σ (sigma).

Finally, the famous Olympic Games began during the archaic period. These were played in honor of Zeus. They were the precursor to our own modern games. Events in these early games included boxing, wrestling, and *pankration*, which combined the two. Athletes also competed in the pentathlon, which consisted of a wrestling match, a foot race, the long jump, the javelin, and the discus. Finally, there was chariot racing. The first Olympic Games took place in 776 BCE. They

This ancient Greek amphora depicts athletes in the Olympic Games.

continued every four years until 393 CE. That year, they were banned by the Roman emperor Theodosius, who believed they were **pagan**.

The Classical Period

Exactly when the classical period began is unclear. Some say it was the start of Athenian **democracy**, in 507 BCE. Others believe it was in 500 BCE, when Greeks in Asia Minor rebelled against their Persian rulers. Still others say it was the Persian invasion in 480 BCE, after which the Delian League was formed. The Delian League was an association of Greek city-states led by the Athenians.

Regardless of when it began, the classical period represented the height of ancient Greek civilization. During this era, Greek politics, philosophy, science, and the arts, which had budded during the archaic period, truly blossomed. Many of Greece's great thinkers lived during the classical period. They included Socrates (circa 470–399 BCE), Plato (ca. 428–348 BCE), and Aristotle (384–322 BCE). These thinkers valued rational thought above all else. They used it to explore and explain the world. Ever since, countless scholars have drawn from their work.

Three of ancient Greece's great thinkers: Socrates, Aristotle, and Plato

Socrates.   Aristotle.   Plato.

Unfortunately, there were many wars during the classical period. Some of these wars were fought between Greece and other empires. For example, the Greeks fought the Persians in the Greco-Persian Wars, which lasted from 490 to 449 BCE. More often, these wars were fought among the Greek city-states themselves. For example, in the Peloponnesian War, Athens fought Sparta from 431 to 404 BCE. In the Corinthian War, from 395 to 387 BCE, Athens, Argos, Thebes, and Corinth joined forces against Sparta. This series of **internecine** wars continued until 338 BCE, when Philip II of Macedon (382–336 BCE) conquered all of Greece except Sparta.

The First Marathon

In 490 BCE, during the first Persian invasion of Greece, a Greek messenger named Pheidippides (ca. 530–490 BCE) ran 25 miles (40.2 kilometers), from Marathon to Athens, to announce that the Greeks had won an important battle. He then collapsed and died. Today, people run races of a similar distance, called marathons, in his honor.

Philip II was murdered in 336 BCE, while at the wedding of his daughter. Philip's son, Alexander III of Macedon (356–323 BCE), ascended the throne. He later became known as Alexander the Great. During Alexander's reign, the Greek empire grew beyond Macedon and Greece to include Asia Minor, Assyria, the Levant, Egypt, Mesopotamia, Media, Persia, Afghanistan, Pakistan, and central Asia. It might have grown even larger if Alexander had not died in Babylon in 323 BCE. He was just thirty-two years old. The cause of his death remains a mystery. Theories range from poisoning to meningitis to a bacterial infection.

The Hellenistic Period

Alexander's death marked the beginning of the Greek Hellenistic period. It also marked a turning point in ancient Greece. Greek culture continued to spread due to Alexander's efforts abroad—although it tended to coexist with, rather than replace, the existing local culture. Greek power and territory, however, waned. This was mainly because Alexander's empire was divided among his three top generals, called the Diadochi, who spent the next forty-plus years fighting among themselves.

Alexander the Great

In an attempt to win back their independence, some Greek city-states formed leagues. For example, Thebes, Corinth, and Argo teamed up to form the Achaean League. Sparta and Athens joined together to form the Aetolian League. However, these leagues often just fought each other or helped one member of the Diadochi in its fight with another.

The end of the Hellenistic period, and of ancient Greece itself, occurred in 146 BCE. That year, much of Greece became a Roman protectorate. This meant it was subject to Roman rule, laws, and, in some cases, taxes. In one last bid for freedom, the Greeks shed the yoke of Roman rule in 88 BCE. However, their independence was short lived. Rome reclaimed Greece in 65 BCE and in 27 BCE, the Roman Empire officially **annexed** Greece.

This marble relief depicts a Greek physician treating a patient's shoulder.

Chapter Two

Advancements in Science

The ancient Greeks made impressive advancements in science, particularly in the areas of mathematics, astronomy, and medicine. This is mainly because of the Greeks' emphasis on evidence-based reasoning and observation. Unlike all civilizations before them—and many since—the ancient Greeks developed a way of understanding the world around them that did not rely on magic, myth, or religion (although the Greeks did worship several deities). This ancient Greek system of logic served as the precursor to the scientific method upon which all modern science relies.

Mathematics

Ancient Greece was not the first civilization to think in mathematical terms. Even people in prehistoric hunter-gatherer societies used numbers. By 2500 BCE, the Babylonians could do multiplication, division, and rudimentary geometry. (The Babylonians used a sexagesimal, or base-60, number system. Today, we see traces of this system in the way we divide minutes into sixty seconds, hours into sixty minutes, and circles into 360 degrees.) Beginning around 2000 BCE, the Egyptians advanced the field of mathematics even further to include fractions, composite and prime numbers, and more. Then, starting around 800 BCE, people in India began exploring the math behind complex geometric shapes.

The Egyptian, Babylonian, and Indus civilizations were largely responsible for the foundation of mathematical thought. However, it was the ancient Greeks, with their emphasis on reason and evidence, who laid out the rules that govern modern mathematics. In fact, the word "mathematics" derives from the Greek *mathema*, or "subject of instruction." Many of the symbols used in modern mathematics, such as pi (∏), sigma (Σ), and delta (Δ), are from the Greek alphabet.

Beginning in the seventh century BCE, the Greeks developed the basic rules of geometry and conceived the formal mathematical proof. They also made discoveries in number theory, mathematical analysis, and applied mathematics. The Greeks were so advanced in the field of mathematics that they nearly invented the complex form of math called integral calculus! Even today, students learn about the discoveries of Greek mathematicians.

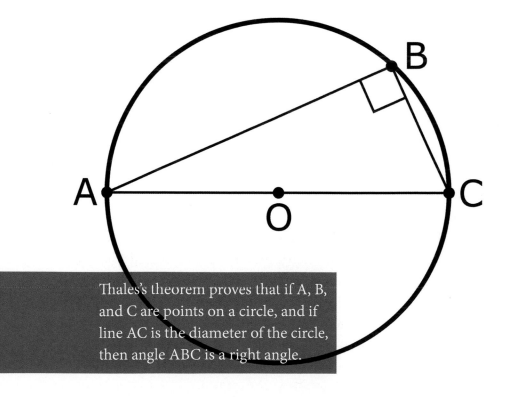

Thales's theorem proves that if A, B, and C are points on a circle, and if line AC is the diameter of the circle, then angle ABC is a right angle.

Thales of Miletus (ca. 624–548 BCE) was the first person to make a mathematical discovery. He is considered the first "true" mathematician. He was also the first person to use geometry to solve certain problems. For example, he discovered how to calculate the height of the pyramids based on the length of their shadows. He also figured out how to determine the distance of a ship from the shore. Thales is credited with the development of the first mathematical theorems. One was Thales's theorem. It proves that if A, B, and C are points on a circle, and if line AC is a diameter of the circle, then angle ABC is a right angle. The other was the intercept theorem. It pertains to the ratios of line segments created when a pair of parallels intercepts two intersecting lines.

A papyrus fragment of Euclid's *Elements*

Another early Greek mathematician, Pythagoras of Samos (ca. 570–495 BCE), founded an order, or group, called the Pythagoreans. This order organized Greek mathematics into a clear, logical system. They believed math was worthy of study in its own right rather than simply for its practical applications. In addition to discovering irrational numbers, the Pythagoreans developed the Pythagorean theorem. It states that the square of the hypotenuse of a right triangle equals the sum of the squares of the other two sides.

Beginning in the fourth century BCE, as Greek culture spread, scholars of Greek mathematics exchanged ideas with authorities in other schools of mathematical thought. This gave rise to what is now called Hellenistic mathematics. During this period, the scholar Euclid, whose precise dates of birth and death are unknown but who lived in Alexandria during the reign of Ptolemy I (323–283 BCE), published *Elements*. This would serve as a primary textbook for mathematicians—especially those studying geometry—until the early twentieth century. It was also during this period that Archimedes of Syracuse (ca. 287–212 BCE) calculated an approximate value of pi.

Astronomy

Thanks in large part to their advancements in mathematics, the ancient Greeks also made significant progress in the field of astronomy. Just as they defined the rules governing modern mathematics, the ancient Greeks used reason and evidence to understand and explain celestial events.

The *Iliad* and the *Odyssey* were two famous epic Greek poems. They originated sometime between 1102 BCE and 850 BCE. Both of these poems mention specific stars and constellations. These include Sirius and Orion, which were identified and named by the ancient Greeks. In fact, Greek astronomers were responsible for the identification and naming of most of the constellations in the northern hemisphere, as well as many stars. These early Greeks were also the first to suggest that Earth was a sphere, and they identified the planets

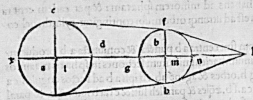

angulum. faciat igitur í ſphæ
ris orbes c d e.f g h. in cono
autem tríangulum c e K.non
dubium quin iuxta f g h. cir
cumferentiam ſit ſectio ſphæ
ræ:cuius baſis eſt circa diame
trum. f h.orbis pars lumine
perfuſa & ſub ſectiöe ea quæ

iuxta c d e:circumferentiam cuius baſis eſt qui circa diametrum c e.orbis rectus exi
ſtens in a b.rectam lineam: etenim f g h.circüferentia lumine perfunditur ſub c.d e.
circumferentia.extrema ſi quidem rądii ſunt c x.e h.eſtꝗ in f g h.ſectione centrum
ſphæræ b.proinde ſphæræ pars lumine perfuſa maior eſt hemiſphærio.

❡In luna mini
mus orbis diſpe
ſcit opacum & lu
cidum cum com
præhendens co
nus & ſolé & lu
naꝫ uerticem ha
buerit ad noſtrú
uiſum. Sit no
ſter uiſus ad a ſo
lis autem centrũ
b lunæ porro cen
ttum cum comp

hendens conus ſolem & lunam uerticem habuerit ad noſtrum uiſum c.cum autem
minus d non dubium quin a c b.in recta ſint línea.educatur per a b & d puncti pla
nurv.Faciet autem ſectiones in ſphæris orbes.at in conis rectas lineas.faciat in ſphæ
ra quoꝗ per quam fertur centrum lunæ orbem c d a.igitur centrum eſt ipſius. nam
id ſupponitur:at in ſole e f r.orbem:ut in luna cum compræhendens conus ſolem
& lunam uerticem habuerit ad noſtrum uiſum orbem h l.Cum autem non m n x.in
conis autem rectas lineas e a.a g.p o.o r.At axes a b.b o.& quia eſt ut ex centro e f g.
orbis ad ex cētro h K l.ita ex cē
tro e f g.orbis ad ex cētro m n x.
uerum ut quæ ex centro e f g or
bis ad ex cētro h l k.orbis.ita b a
ad a c.ut aũt ex cētro e f g. orbis
ad ex centro m n x. orbis.ita eſt
b o.ad o d. & ut igit b a ad a c.
ita b o.ad o d.& diſtribatim ut b

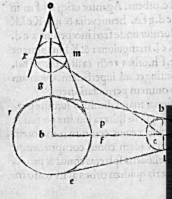

h k l.

The Antikythera Mechanism

In 1900, Greek sponge divers discovered a strange machine. They found it among the remains of a shipwreck off the coast of the Greek island Antikythera. Likely built in the second century BCE, the so-called Antikythera mechanism was designed to predict astronomical positions and eclipses. It is considered the first **analog computer**.

The machine, housed in a wooden casing, was a complex clock mechanism. It had at least thirty gears. The front face of the mechanism had a fixed-ring dial that showed the **ecliptic**. The ecliptic is the path of the sun on the celestial sphere. Another ring outside the fixed ring—this one movable—marked the months

The Antikythera mechanism is considered the world's first analog computer.

and days of the Egyptian calendar. These were written in Greek and accompanied by their corresponding Zodiac symbols.

To use the mechanism, you rotated the movable ring to line up with the current point in the ecliptic. Then, using a hand crank, you moved a pointer on the dial to point to the correct day in the Egyptian calendar. This caused the complex system of small gears inside the mechanism to rotate. Through the rotation of these gears, the device calculated the position of the sun and moon and perhaps even the planets.

It also calculated the moon phase, eclipse, and calendar cycles. These were revealed by five dials on the back of the device. One cycle was the Metonic cycle. It comprises 235 synodic months, or lunar phases—almost a common multiple of the solar year and the lunar month. Another cycle was the Callippic cycle. This is a cycle of 76 years. It was proposed in 330 BCE as an improvement over the Metonic cycle. Third was the Saros cycle. Consisting of approximately 223 synodic months, this cycle was used to predict both solar and lunar eclipses. The Exeligmos cycle was fourth. This cycle is a period of 54 years and 33 days. Like the Saros cycle, the Exeligmos cycle was used to predict solar and lunar eclipses. Finally, the machine tracked the Olympiad cycle. This was a four-year cycle, reflecting the regularity with which the ancient Olympic Games occurred.

Scientists later determined that the machine's calculations were slightly off. Still, the mechanism remains an amazing feat of mathematics and engineering for its time. Indeed, experts claim that its level of complexity and workmanship rivaled that of the astronomical clocks that emerged in Europe some 1,500 years later.

that are visible to the naked eye: Mercury, Venus, Mars, Jupiter, and Saturn. Indeed, the word "planet" comes from the Greek *planetes*, which means "wanderer." This speaks to the way the planets move across the night sky.

During the fourth century BCE, Greek scholars developed a three-dimensional model to explain the motion of the planets. They also correctly theorized that the earth rotated on an axis. During the third century BCE, Greek scholars correctly concluded that Earth was part of a **heliocentric system**. In other words, it revolved around the sun rather than the other way around. They also accurately estimated the circumference of Earth, the sun, and the moon, as well as the distance of the sun and moon from Earth. In the second century BCE, the ancient Greeks compiled a star catalog. In this catalog, they recorded not only the presence and position of each star, but also its level of brilliance. That way, later generations could determine whether a given star had moved, changed in intensity, or died out.

The ancient Greeks recognized the infinite nature of space. They also suggested there might be more than one solar system. This **hypothesis** was put forth by Democritus (ca. 460–370 BCE). Metrodotus of Chios, whose dates of birth and death are unknown, agreed with this hypothesis, observing, "A single ear of wheat in a large field is as strange as a single world in infinite space."

Medicine

As with most ancient people, the life-span of ancient Greeks was relatively short. This was especially true before and during the archaic period. Half of all children in ancient Greece died before their tenth birthday, and one in three perished in infancy. People who did live to adulthood tended to survive only into their forties or fifties.

At first, the early Greeks believed illness and disease were punishment from the gods. Conversely, they thought healing was a gift from the gods (although the *Iliad* does contain references to the

The rod of Asclepius

The rod of Asclepius features a staff with a snake wrapped around it. This has long been a symbol of medicine. Even today, it appears in the logos of several important medical organizations. These include the American Medical Association, the American Veterinary Medical Association, and the Blue Cross Blue Shield Association. It's also featured in the Star of Life, which appears on many ambulances.

use of herbs, bandages, and wine to treat battle wounds, as well as attempts to perform rudimentary surgery). This view was so pervasive that the Greeks even worshipped a god of medicine. This god was named Asclepius. To honor this god, the early Greeks built special temples called Asclepieia. These doubled as basic medical clinics.

Eventually, Greek scholars began to apply reason and evidence to the field of medicine, much as they had with mathematics and astronomy. This resulted in a more scientific approach to the practice of medicine. In 700 BCE, the Greeks built their first medical school, in Cnidus (now modern-day Turkey). This school established the practice of carefully observing patients. It also produced the first anatomical charts.

Around 460 BCE, Hippocrates was born. He would later be called the "father of modern medicine." Hippocrates, who was himself the son of a physician, founded a medical school at Kos. He and his students collected about seventy medical works into what they called the *Hippocratic Corpus*. This collection documented many illnesses and best practices for physicians. The *Hippocratic Corpus* included a treatise called *The Sacred Disease*. This treatise challenged the idea that illness was a form of divine punishment. After all, if that were the case, then the medical treatments developed by humankind would be ineffective. Another treatise, *Of the Epidemics*, discussed the importance of the relationship between the patient and the physician. It said, "The art [medicine] consists in three things—the disease, the patient, and the physician … The physician is the servant of the art, and the patient must combat the disease along with the physician." Perhaps the most significant contribution of Hippocrates was the development of the Hippocratic oath, which physicians take even today. This oath, long considered a rite of passage, holds physicians to certain ethical standards.

A bust of Hippocrates. Hippocrates conceived the Hippocratic oath, still sworn by physicians today.

6131
CARNEADE (?)
FARNESE

Thanks to Herophilus of Chalcedon (ca. 335–280 BCE), who performed many dissections on the human body as well as on animals, the Greeks learned a lot about human anatomy. Herophilus mapped the veins, arteries, and nerves in the body. He also studied the brain, eyes, liver, pancreas, salivary glands, and reproductive system. He first identified the difference between veins and arteries, concluding that both were filled with blood. (Previously, the Greeks believed they contained a mixture of blood, air, and water.) He was also the first to measure the pulse and to use this measurement as a tool to diagnose certain conditions.

Herophilus conducted many of his dissections on living subjects. This practice is called **vivisection**. Typically, the subjects of his dissections were criminals. As noted by historian Jonathan Barnes, "[W]hile they were still breathing [Herophilus and his colleague] observed parts which nature had formerly concealed, and examined their position, colour, shape, size, arrangement, hardness, softness, smoothness, connection."

The last of the great early Greek physicians was Galen (ca. 129–216 CE). Galen lived under Roman rule but was of Greek lineage. By Galen's time, the practice of human dissection had been outlawed. However, Galen learned a lot about human anatomy by tending to injured gladiators. He also explored the use of minerals and herbs for medicinal purposes to treat both physical and mental ailments, and he was the first to write down the ingredients of his prescriptions. Galen wrote more than three hundred books and papers. Sadly, many were destroyed in a fire.

Humoral Medicine

Early Greek physicians, including Hippocrates, practiced humoral medicine. That is, they believed the body was composed of four humors. These humors were blood, yellow bile, black bile, and phlegm. If these humors fell out of balance, the result was illness or disease. It was the job of the physician to restore the balance of these four humors.

How did the humors fall out of balance? Greek doctors believed this sometimes occurred because of the patient's living conditions. They observed more instances of illness and disease among patients faced with mosquitoes, rats, and dirty drinking water. Diet, they thought, was another factor. So was physical trauma, such as that suffered by warriors. Greek doctors also believed the patient's mindset played a role, along with his or her gender.

The ancient Greeks' view of the body was incorrect. Still, they managed to identify various factors that contributed to illness. But the Greeks' *real* contribution to medicine was simply the notion that the human body was something that could be understood at all.

Remnants of the ancient Athenian civilization can still be seen in modern-day Athens.

Chapter Three

Democracy

Today, Greece is one nation, but this was not always the case. As you learned in chapter 1, ancient Greece was in fact divided into several small city-states. The Greeks called these *poleis*. (*Poleis* is the plural form of *polis*.) One Greek city-state was Athens. Another was Sparta. Thebes, Rhodes, and Syracuse are yet more examples.

Polis in Modern Language

In modern times, the word *polis* often appears in the names of cities. Examples include Minneapolis, Indianapolis, Annapolis, and so on. It also appears in words that describe urban areas, such as metropolis, megalopolis, and cosmopolis. (And don't forget necropolis, which means city of the dead—another way of saying cemetery or graveyard!) Finally, polis is the root of the words policy, politics, and police.

The ancient Greeks were bound by a common language, religion, and culture. Still, each city-state was distinct from the others. Every city-state had its own customs, festivals, laws, government, coinage, and armed forces.

When faced with a common threat, the Greek city-states might band together to form leagues. For example, the Delian League formed in 481 BCE to fend off the Persians. But once the threat had passed, these leagues often dissolved.

Democracy Defined

Historians say the Greek city-states started out as kingdoms. Later, many became **oligarchies**. Eventually, one city-state, Athens, adopted an entirely new form of government: *demokratia*, or democracy. This meant "rule by the people." Like many aspects of Athenian life, democracy eventually had its own deity, a goddess named Demokratia.

Pericles (ca. 495–429 BCE), an Athenian general, described democracy as putting power "in the hands not of a minority but of the whole people." Pericles continued, "When it is a question of settling private disputes, everyone is equal before the law; when it is a question of putting one person before another in positions of public responsibility, what counts is not membership of a particular class, but the actual ability which the man possesses." He concluded, "No one, so long as he has it in him to be of service to the state, is kept in political obscurity because of poverty."

Democracy in one form or another soon spread from Athens to many other Greek city-states. Sparta was one notable holdout. During the period when democracy flourished in Athens and abroad, Sparta stubbornly remained a monarchy—or, more precisely, a dyarchy, ruled by two hereditary monarchs.

The Birth of Democracy

Democracy came about in phases. In 620 BCE, Draco, the ruler of Athens, whose dates of birth and death are unknown, developed a written constitution. This constitution was displayed on wooden tablets. It documented many of the existing oral laws. Unfortunately, these laws mainly served the interest of the Athenian aristocracy.

Worse, they were terribly harsh. Greek citizens could be sentenced to death for infractions as minor as stealing an apple or a cabbage. Even today, people describe laws that are very harsh as "draconian."

In 594 BCE, the new ruler of Athens, Solon, overturned the Draconian constitution (although he did preserve the Draconian laws pertaining to homicide), replacing it with one of his own. This Solonian constitution, written in poetic form, put into place at least some protections for the poor. For example, in an attempt to protect poor Athenians from falling into slavery, the Solonian constitution banned lenders from granting loans using people's freedom as collateral, and it freed existing debt-slaves. This constitution also gave all Athenians, rich or poor, the right to appeal to a jury. (Solon's trial by jury system was the first of its kind—yet another contribution by the ancient Greeks to the modern world!) That's not to say the poor were *equal* with the rich under Solon. They weren't. Solon divided the citizenry into four classes based on land ownership, and those in the lower classes were not allowed to perform certain government functions. Still, the poor were better off than they were before.

Sadly, the Athenian rulers who followed Solon were less enlightened. Many could only be described as tyrants. That changed in 508 BCE when Cleisthenes (ca. 570–508 BCE) rose to power after the removal of a tyrant named Isagoras. Cleisthenes changed the Athenian constitution yet again, instituting reforms to end tyranny for good. These reforms represented ancient Greece's first real step toward democracy.

First, Cleisthenes reorganized the citizenry. As mentioned, Solon had divided it into four main classes. Cleisthenes mixed these four main classes into ten groups. What group you were in depended on what part of the polis you lived in. This was called your deme. By mingling the members of the four classes, Cleisthenes effectively stripped the wealthiest citizens of their power.

In this relief, the goddess Demokratia (*right*), representing democracy, crowns Demos (*left*), representing the demes.

Next, Cleisthenes established a practice called sortition. With sortition, many government positions were appointed by lottery from a pool of eligible citizens. This was quite different from the old way of filling these posts: assigning them to members of a leader's family or social group. (It is also quite different from how such positions are filled in modern-day democracies, which rely on elections or appointments.)

A bust of Cleisthenes. His constitution represented ancient Greece's first real step toward democracy.

The Branches of Athenian Democracy

Under Cleisthenes, the government of Athens consisted of three branches, much like the government of the United States does now. And like the United States government, the Athenian system allowed for checks and balances, thereby reducing the likelihood of an abuse of power. Cleisthenes did not form these three branches of government. They existed before his rise to power. He did, however, change their rules to be more inclusive of *all* male citizens—not just the wealthy few.

One branch of Athenian government was the *boule*. Members of this representative body—fifty from each deme, or five hundred in all—were chosen by lottery and served for a period of one year. That way, no single individual or group could grow too powerful. The boule convened on a daily basis to handle much of the Athenian government's routine business. In addition, it was the job of the boule to propose bills or laws on which a second branch of the government, the *ekklesia*, would vote.

The ancient Greeks used *ostraka* to cast their vote in a secret ballot.

The Bouleutic Oath

New members of the boule were expected to swear an oath, called the bouleutic oath. The precise contents of this oath are lost to history. One source, Lysias (ca. 445–380 BCE), said members of the boule swore to "advise what was best for the city." Another, Xenophon (ca. 430–354 BCE), alleged they vowed to "advise according to the laws." Still another, Demosthenes (384–322 BCE), held that they promised to do "what was best for the people." It may have been the case that the oath evolved over time, meaning all three men were correct.

The ekklesia, or assembly, was open to all forty-thousand-odd eligible male citizens—although typically, only about five thousand attended any given session. It met forty times per year to vote on laws proposed by the boule. If a majority approved a measure, the measure passed. If not, it failed. The ekklesia also dictated foreign policy, declared war, and set military strategy. Finally, it elected certain high-ranking magistrates, called *archontes*, who performed important government functions, and generals, called *strategoi*, who led military campaigns.

Typically, members of the ekklesia voted by show of hands. In some instances, however—like when voting on whether to **ostracize** a particular Athenian citizen (for, say, conspiring against the government or committing some other offense), secret ballot was the preferred method. In that case, the members of the assembly marked their vote on a piece of broken pottery, called an *ostrakon*.

The third branch of Athenian government was the *dikasteria*. These were the courts of law. Here, citizens argued cases before a jury of male citizens over the age of thirty. Like the members of the boule, these jurors, called *dikastai*, were selected by lottery. (This happened on a daily, rather than yearly, basis.) Unlike juries of today,

Part of the ancient Acropolis in Athens. The Acropolis was the center of the city-state's athletic, artistic, spiritual, and political life.

which typically consist of a dozen people, early Athenian juries had 500, 1,000, or even 1,500 dikastai, depending on the case. The dikastai were not expected to reach a unanimous decision. A simple majority, taken by secret ballot, was all that was required. According to Aristotle, the dikasteria "contributed most to the strength of democracy."

Problems with Athenian Democracy

The Athenians expected all eligible men to participate in the political process. However, this was not always possible. Some men were away, serving in the Athenian army or navy. Others could not afford to take time off from work. As a result, participants in the various governmental branches tended to tilt toward the wealthy elite. That meant the government did not *truly* reflect the will of the people. Another concern with Athenian democracy was that although the system was designed to prevent conspiracies, they did sometimes arise. Also, some citizens were easily swayed by talented orators or charismatic leaders, and those less-educated members of the populace often lacked the knowledge they needed to make good decisions. To counteract this, Plato wrote, "The organization of the city must be confided to those who possess knowledge, who alone can enable their fellow-citizens to attain virtue, and therefore excellence, by means of education."

The End of Athenian Democracy

Enlightened though it was, Athenian democracy was doomed to failure—at least in ancient Greece. What happened? In 413 BCE, the Athenians suffered a costly defeat in Sicily during the Peloponnesian War. (This war was between Athens and the Peloponnesian League, led by Sparta.) The loss—two hundred ships, thirty thousand oarsmen, and ten thousand soldiers—was devastating. And of course, there were financial repercussions. Years of fighting had emptied Athens's treasury. In an attempt to take control of the city's finances and influence the outcome of the war, a group of prominent Athenians launched a coup in 411 BCE. They overthrew the government and installed an oligarchy, called the Four Hundred.

Despite the efforts of the oligarchs, Athens fell to Sparta in 404 BCE. This marked the end of the war. Sparta immediately installed its own tyrannical regime in Athens, called the Thirty Tyrants. But in 403 BCE, the Athenians, led by a general named Thrasybulus (440–388 BCE), overthrew it. Democracy was restored—and would remain until 338 BCE, when Philip II of Macedon conquered all of Greece except Sparta.

An ancient Greek theater in Sicily

Chapter Four

Architecture, Theater, and Weaponry

The contributions of the ancient Greeks span far beyond science and democracy. These incredible people made considerable advancements in areas as varied as architecture, theater, and weaponry.

Architecture

Thanks to their significant advancements in mathematics, the ancient Greeks made several important contributions to the field of architecture. One was their discovery of the **golden ratio**. Two values are said to be in a golden ratio if the ratio of the two values equals

The Crane and the Wheelbarrow

Stone was the main building material in ancient Greece. But stone is heavy. This makes it hard to transport. To help with this, the ancient Greeks invented the crane. They used this to hoist large pieces of stone into place. The ancient Greeks also invented the wheelbarrow to help move building materials. With a wheelbarrow, each worker could transport more than twice what he could carry by hand—and with much less effort!

the ratio of the sum of the two values to the larger of the two values. Ancient Greek architects used this ratio to calculate the proportions of buildings. The ratio created a sense of balance, making the buildings most pleasing to the eye.

Greek architects also used complicated calculations to tweak the viewer's perspective of a building. For example, they often designed the building's outermost columns to lean slightly inward. They also positioned them more closely together than the others. This technique is famously evident in the Parthenon, in Athens. It was built during the fifth century BCE as a temple for the goddess Athena.

The Parthenon was just one temple built by the ancient Greeks. Countless others were constructed. Each honored a particular god or goddess. As mentioned, the Parthenon honored the goddess Athena. Others were devoted to Zeus, Poseidon, Apollo, or any number of other Greek deities. Greek architects designed most of these temples to be in harmony with the landscape around them. Often, they were built

The Parthenon in Athens

on high ground, for emphasis. Sometimes, they were oriented to face certain stars or constellations. To make sure the building would last, ancient Greek architects also surveyed the proposed site. They used special tools to assess the soil and gauge the slope of the ground.

Most Greek temples were rectangular in shape. Usually, they were about twice as long as they were wide. A few were quite large—well over 300 feet (91 meters) long. Inside was a statue of the god or goddess for whom the temple was built. Nearly every Greek temple was constructed of stone—often limestone or marble.

Heating and Plumbing

The ancient Greeks made important innovations in heating and plumbing. This greatly improved their lives. Evidence of central heating appears in many Greek temples. One is the Temple of Artemis in Ephesus. In addition, excavations throughout Greece have revealed extensive plumbing systems. These systems served public baths, fountains, and even some homes.

Most temples shared certain design elements. One was a base called the *crepidoma*. Typically, the crepidoma consisted of three steps (although some temples had more). The top step, called the *stylobate*, supported a series of stone columns. These defined the perimeter of the structure. Lintels, or beams, lay across the tops of the columns to connect them. Above the lintels was an **entablature**. This supported the roof. The temple's walls were typically made of large stone blocks.

Ancient Greek architecture is divided into three separate orders: Doric, Ionic, and Corinthian. Each order had its own features and characteristics. These features and characteristics were often evident in the appearance of a building's columns.

Doric columns were the simplest and plainest of the three. The capital of a Doric column—that is, the piece at the top—looks like a simple circular cushion. In contrast, columns of the Ionic order—the

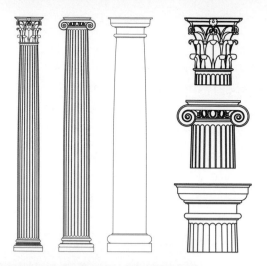

From left to right and top to bottom: Corinthian, Ionic, and Doric columns

slenderest of the three—feature a volute, or scroll-like decoration, on the capital. Corinthian columns are even more ornate. Their capitals feature leaves and scrolls.

Of course, the ancient Greeks built more than just temples. They also built open-air theaters, town halls, public baths, gymnasiums, and even stadiums. One famous stadium was the Panathenaic Stadium, in Athens. First built in 329 BCE, it held roughly forty-five thousand people. The Panathenaic Stadium was later restored for use in the 1896, 1906, and 2004 Olympic Games. And of course, the Greeks built private homes.

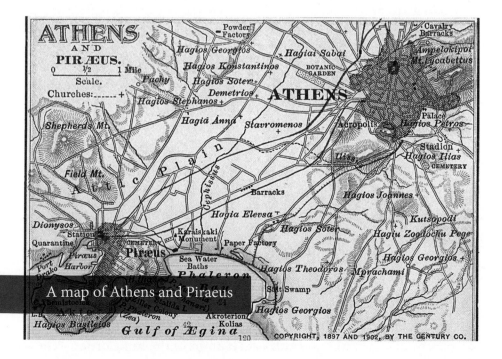

A map of Athens and Piraeus

Urban Planning

The ancient Greeks were among the first to do urban planning. Hippodamus of Miletus (498–408 BCE) was the father of urban planning. He believed that creating an orderly urban environment could positively affect the social order. To create such an environment, Hippodamus designed towns with wide, straight streets that intersected at right angles. The result was a grid pattern. Magna, Piraeus, Rhodes, and Thurium were all designed by Hippodamus. Even today, new cities and towns are planned using this same grid pattern.

Greek architecture had a significant effect on the architecture of societies that followed. One can easily see its influence on Roman architecture. In addition, ancient Greek architecture served as the basis for the Greek revival and neoclassical architectural movements during the eighteenth and nineteenth centuries. Even today, architects look to the ancient Greeks for inspiration and ideas.

Theater

Many ancient Greek towns had an open-air theater. These theaters were typically set into a hillside and featured tiered seating for as many as fourteen thousand people. The seats were set in a semicircle and faced a circular performance space called the orchestra. These were the first theaters ever constructed on Earth. Indeed, the word "theater" comes from the ancient Greek *theatron*, or "watching place." Ancient Greek theaters had amazing acoustics. Even audience members who sat in the very top row could hear the actors' voices. This was not by accident. The Greeks used complex calculations to determine the best shape for the theater for maximum volume.

Interestingly, the earliest known theatrical event did not occur in Greece. Rather, it took place in Egypt, around 2000 BCE. There are also references to theatrical productions in China as early as 1500 BCE. But it was the ancient Greeks who elevated theater into an art form.

The very earliest Greek plays had just one actor, called the protagonist, and a **chorus**. The chorus was a group of performers whose role was to comment on the action. Members of the chorus often wore masks. The first of these plays was performed around 532 BCE, by the first known actor, Thespis. Even today, people use the term "thespian," derived from Thespis, to refer to an actor. Eventually, a playwright named Aeschylus (ca. 525–456 BCE) introduced a second role, called the antagonist, to add conflict. In doing so, Aeschylus essentially invented dialogue and conceived of the notion of "drama."

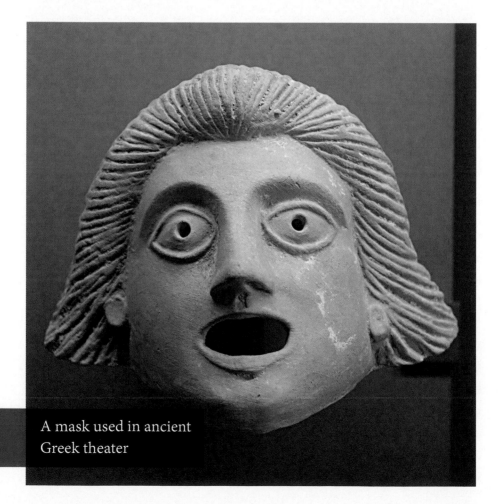

A mask used in ancient Greek theater

After Aeschylus came Sophocles (ca. 497–406 BCE). Sophocles added a third actor to the mix, called the tritagonist. The tritagonist minimized the significance of the chorus in Greek theater. Sophocles also introduced the concept of irony to Greek theater. Irony figures prominently in his most famous play, *Oedipus Rex* or *Oedipus the King*. This play tells the story of Oedipus, who was abandoned by his parents at birth. Oedipus becomes king by unknowingly fulfilling a prophecy that he would murder his father, Laius, and marry his mother, Jocasta. One example of irony in *Oedipus Rex* is when Oedipus demands that whoever murdered Laius be punished, unaware that he is that man. Another is when Oedipus ridicules the oracle Tiresius for being blind, when it is Oedipus who lacks sight (metaphorically speaking).

The Persians

A play by Aeschylus called *The Persians*, written in 476 BCE, is the oldest surviving Greek play. It recounted the defeat of Persian ruler Xerxes at the hand of the Greeks. It was the second play in a trilogy. The first, *Phineus*, related the rescue of King Phineus by Jason and the Argonauts. The third, *Glaucus*, may have centered on a Corinthian king named Glaucus, who was eaten by his own horses. Or it might have told the tale of a farmer named Glaucus, who changed into a sea god after eating a magical herb. No copies of these plays remain.

A third ancient playwright, Euripides (ca. 480–406 BCE), invented the prologue to introduce the story. He also invented the deus ex machina, a theatrical device used to wrap up loose ends. Euripides wrote plays that questioned societal norms about "men and women [who] destroy each other by the intensity of their loves and hates." One such play by Euripides was *Medea*. It was about a barbarian woman named Medea who is married to Jason, of Argonaut fame. When Jason leaves Medea for a Greek princess, Medea murders his new bride. She also kills her own two sons, fathered by Jason, in an effort to destroy him. At the end of the play, Medea escapes to Athens, where she begins a new life. The ancient Greeks found this play shocking. Still, it remains one of the most frequently performed Greek plays in modern times.

Aeschylus, Sophocles, and Euripides wrote tragedies, or plays about human suffering. But another playwright, Aristophanes (ca. 446–386 BCE), soon developed a new type of play: the comedy. As Aristotle explained in his book *Poetics*, comedy is a "representation … of people who are inferior but not wholly vicious: the ridiculous is one category of the embarrassing." Aristotle continued, "What is ridiculous is some error or embarrassment that is neither painful nor life-threatening."

The Evolution of Stagecraft

As plays evolved, so too did the spaces in which they were performed. Beginning in 465 BCE, Greek plays incorporated a backdrop called a *skênê*. This depicted the setting of the play. It also allowed the actors privacy when changing costumes. By 425 BCE, the stage had evolved even further to include a *paraskenia*, or projecting sides. These sometimes had doorways, allowing the actors to enter and exit the stage. Also added was the *proskenion*, which depicted the front of the scene. Many Greek elements of stagecraft are still used today.

Weapons

As discussed in chapter 1 and chapter 3, ancient Greece was not one single nation. Instead, it was composed of several city-states—most notably, Athens and Sparta. Not surprisingly, these city-states did not always get along. Often they found themselves at war. This drove the development of new and deadlier weapons. These included the crossbow, the catapult, and the cannon.

No one knows exactly when the Greeks invented the crossbow, but scholars believe it was sometime before 399 BCE. The Chinese also invented a crossbow of sorts, perhaps as early as 2000 BCE. But it differed in its design from that of the Greeks. This suggests that each civilization developed the weapon independently of the other.

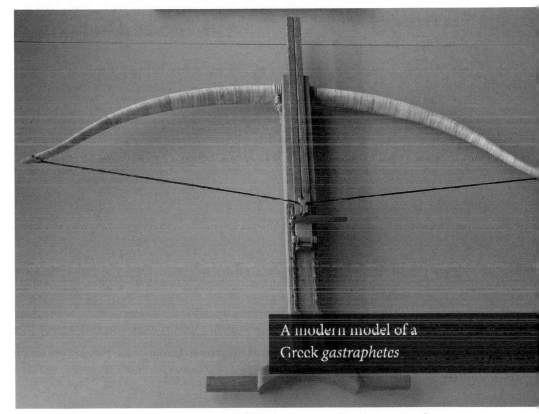

A modern model of a Greek *gastraphetes*

The first known type of Greek crossbow was called a *gastraphetes*. This was similar to the more traditional bow, which had long been used to shoot arrows. The crossbow, however, had more power than the traditional bow. This made it effective even against an armored enemy. It also enabled the archer to shoot arrows much farther. This was true even if the archer was of average strength and size. Soon, the Greeks invented a larger version of the gastraphetes, called an *oxybeles*. This was used to break down enemy walls. Unlike the gastraphetes, the oxybeles was mounted on a tripod and used a winch (also invented by the ancient Greeks). Eventually, the Greeks developed a third type of crossbow, called a *ballista*. This weapon was smaller than the gastraphetes. It had a torsion spring (yet another Greek invention), which allowed it to shoot both faster and farther.

From the crossbow came the *katapeltikon*, or catapult. This weapon represented an attempt by the ancient Greeks to increase the size, range, and power of their crossbow-style weapons. As such, it was considerably larger and required multiple people to operate. According to the Greek historian Diodorus Sicilus, who lived during the first century BCE, this weapon was invented in 399 BCE. Like the ballista before it, the katapeltikon relied on torsion springs. The size of these springs was directly proportional to the size of the catapult and the intended projectile. At first, the katapeltikon shot arrows. Later, it evolved to shoot rocks. Sometimes, for added effect, these projectiles were set on fire.

Archimedes of Syracuse invented the first cannon. He was a famous mathematician who also calculated an accurate approximation of pi. Archimedes designed the cannon, which was made of wood, in an attempt to defend his city against the Romans during the Siege of Syracuse. This cannon drew from the field of pneumatics, the study of gases, first explored by Ctesibius of Alexandria (285–222 BCE). The cannon used heat and water to produce steam. This generated enough pressure to hurl a projectile from the bore of the cannon toward a target. Sadly, the Romans slew Archimedes after overrunning the city, despite orders from the Roman general to spare his life. Still, Archimedes's invention lived on.

Relics of the ancient Greek
civilization survive in
modern times.

Chapter Five

The Legacy of Ancient Greece

As mentioned in chapter 1, Greece became a protectorate of Rome in 146 BCE, but the Roman Empire itself fell in 465 CE—or at least the portion of the empire that spanned western Europe. One consequence of this collapse was that the knowledge gained by both the Greeks and the Romans—in mathematics and medicine, in architecture, astronomy, and the arts—was lost to the Western world.

Fortunately, the eastern part of the Roman Empire, in and around Constantinople (now called Istanbul), remained intact. The Romans in this region, later called the Byzantines, preserved and even built upon much of this "lost" knowledge. The reintroduction of this knowledge to western Europe would bring sweeping and lasting changes.

The Rebirth of Greek Culture

In 1453 CE, Ottoman Turks overran the city of Constantinople. This city was the heart of the Byzantine Empire. This caused the Byzantine Empire to collapse.

After the collapse, many Byzantine scholars moved to western Europe. When they did, they brought with them what knowledge their society had preserved. This included knowledge gained by the ancient Greeks, which had long been lost to western Europe.

The reintroduction of this knowledge to western Europe by the Byzantines spurred massive change. Indeed, many scholars say this event caused the end of Europe's Middle Ages. The Middle Ages were described as a "time of ignorance and superstition" that favored "the word of religious authorities over personal experience and rational activity." What followed was a period known as the Renaissance. The word "Renaissance" translates to "rebirth." Indeed, there *was* a rebirth—a rebirth of Greek culture.

What Was Lost

In her famous book *The Greek Way*, Greek scholar Edith Hamilton (1867–1963 CE) wrote, "Of all that the Greeks did only a very small part has come down to us and we have no means of knowing if we have their best … Little is left of all this wealth of great art: the sculptures defaced and broken into bits have crumbled away; the buildings are fallen; the paintings gone forever; of the writings, all lost but a very few. We have only the ruin of what was." Hamilton had a point. Yes, the frescoes of the Minoans remain. So too does the occasional written play. And yes, the Parthenon still stands, as do many other ancient Greek structures. But how many more frescoes, plays, and buildings were lost? How many works of art or scraps of knowledge are gone forever? We can never know.

The Stamp of Ancient Greek Culture

Even without those missing pieces, the ancient Greeks left a lasting legacy. As noted by Edith Hamilton, "This little remnant preserved by the haphazard of chance shows the high-water mark reached in every region of thought and beauty the Greeks entered … No sculpture comparable to theirs; no buildings more beautiful; no writings superior." The "stamp" of the ancient Greeks, Hamilton wrote, "is upon all of the art and all of the thought of the Western world."

Where do we see this stamp of the ancient Greeks in the modern world? Consider the innovations discussed in this book alone. Today's mathematicians still rely on mathematical concepts and theories that were first developed by the ancient Greeks. As for astronomy, the ancient Greeks' observations about the shape of Earth, the location of various stars and planets, and the heliocentric nature of our solar system informed navigators for centuries. Indeed, these observations are the foundation on which modern-day space exploration was built. And although the ancient Greeks were wrong about the workings of the human body—it was not, as they believed, composed of four humors—they made considerable advancements in the *practice* of medicine. Specifically, the ancient Greeks understood the importance of observation, and that illness was not the result of some divine punishment.

In the area of architecture, many buildings constructed during modern times have traces of the ancient Greeks. Many of these can be found in Washington, DC. One example is the Supreme Court Building. Made of white marble, this building has Corinthian columns, an elaborate entablature, and statues in the Greek style. Another example is the US Capitol Building. Although this building's famous dome is more Roman in style, its countless columns are a variation on the Corinthian order. And like the columns of the Parthenon, the columns of the Lincoln Memorial incline slightly toward the building's interior. This is to trick the viewer's perspective.

That's not all. Greek weapons such as the crossbow still exist today, although they are used more for sport than for war. Greek theater continues to influence modern works of art. Some Greek plays, such as *Elektra* by Sophocles, have been made into operas. Others have inspired contemporary films. And of course, theater troupes continue to perform original Greek plays, such as *Oedipus Rex*.

Perhaps the most important legacy of the ancient Greeks is democracy. It's true that democracy did not last in ancient Greece. Still, its processes and ideals have lived on.

A modern-day performance of the opera *Elektra* by Richard Strauss, based on the ancient Greek play of the same name

Athenian democracy was, in the words of Pericles, "a unique and truly revolutionary system that realized its basic principle to an unprecedented and quite extreme extent ... No *polis* had ever dared to give all its citizens equal political rights, regardless of their descent, wealth, social standing, education, personal qualities, and any other factors that usually determined status in a community."

In modern times, many societies have adopted democracy in one form or another. The first of these was the United States. After it gained its independence from Britain, the United States formed its own democratic government. Close on the heels of the United States was France. It became a democracy after the French Revolution.

Since then, the notion of "government of the people, by the people, for the people," to quote Abraham Lincoln, has continued to spread. As of 2013, 123 countries (out of 192) are democratic. According to the US State Department, this is good news. Democratic countries, it says, are more likely to "secure the peace, deter aggression, expand open markets, promote economic development, protect American citizens, combat international terrorism and crime, uphold human and worker rights, avoid humanitarian crises and refugee flows, improve the global environment, and protect human health."

It's no wonder historians often refer to ancient Greece as the "cradle of Western civilization." As historian Will Durant wrote in 1939, "There is hardly anything secular in our culture that does not come from Greece." Conversely, "There is nothing in Greek civilization that doesn't illuminate our own."

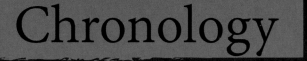

3000 BCE The advent of the Minoan civilization, a precursor to ancient Greek culture. It would endure until 1400 BCE.

1600 BCE The birth of the Mycenaean civilization. It would die out in 1100 BCE.

900 BCE The Greek "dark age" ends with the return of written records. This marks the beginning of the archaic period.

776 BCE The first Olympic Games take place.

507 BCE Cleisthenes rewrites the Athenian constitution, taking the first real steps toward democracy. Some scholars say this marks the end of the archaic period and the beginning of the classical period.

470 BCE Socrates is born.

431 BCE The Peloponnesian War breaks out.

428 BCE Plato is born.

411 BCE Democracy ends in Athens.

399 BCE An Athenian jury condemns Socrates to death.

384 BCE Aristotle is born.

338 BCE Philip II of Macedon conquers much of ancient Greece.

336 BCE Philip II is assassinated. His son, Alexander the Great, succeeds him.

323 BCE Alexander the Great dies after claiming significant territory for his empire. His death marks the end of the classical period and the beginning of the Hellenistic period.

301 BCE Euclid publishes *Elements*.

146 BCE The Romans conquer Greece.

27 BCE The Roman Empire officially annexes Greece.

1453 CE Ottoman Turks invade Constantinople, prompting Byzantine scholars to migrate to western Europe. In this way, the "lost" knowledge of the ancient Greeks is restored to the West.

Glossary

analog computer A computing machine that performs arithmetical operations using some variable physical quantity, such as mechanical movement.

annex To take possession of or appropriate territory.

chorus A group of performers in a Greek play that speaks and moves together. The chorus comments on the action of the play.

city-state A city that has its own government and is its own state.

democracy A system of government that is run by the people.

ecliptic The apparent path of the sun.

entablature An architectural element that holds up the roof of a building.

fresco (plural **frescoes**) A type of painting. Frescoes are made by painting on wet plaster. When the plaster dries, the colors become fixed.

golden ratio A ratio used to calculate proportions. Two values are said to be in a golden ratio if the ratio of the two values equals the ratio of the sum of the two values to the larger of the two values.

heliocentric system An astronomical model in which planets or other astronomical bodies rotate around the sun, rather than the other way around. Our solar system is a heliocentric system.

hypothesis An educated guess that explains how something works. A hypothesis typically leads to further study or discussion.

internecine Describes a clash within a single group or people.

oligarchy A government ruled by a select few influential people. The word is also used to describe the rulers themselves.

ostracize In general terms, to shun from society or a group. In ancient Greece, to ostracize someone meant to banish or exile them.

pagan Describes a religion that is outside the mainstream. Historically, Christians have considered the ancient Greek religion to be pagan.

polytheistic Believing in many gods rather than just one.

vivisection The practice of dissecting or performing operations on a live subject.

Further Information

Books

Garland, Robert. *Ancient Greece: Everyday Life in the Birthplace of Western Civilization*. New York: Sterling Publishing, 2013.

Goldberg, Herbert. *Hippocrates: Father of Medicine*. Lincoln, NE: Authors Choice Press, 2006.

Macdonald, Fiona, and Mark Bergin. *A Greek Temple*. New York: Peter Bedrick Books, 2002.

Osborne, Mary Pope. *Tales from the Odyssey, Parts 1 and 2*. New York: Disney Hyperion, 2012.

Pearson, Anne. *Ancient Greece*. DK Eyewitness Books. New York: DK Children, 2014.

Peterson, Christine. *Greece*. True Books. New York: Children's Press, 2002.

Rodgers, Nigel. *The Complete Illustrated Encyclopedia of Ancient Greece*. London: Lorenz Books, 2014.

Woods, Michael, and Mary B. Woods. *Seven Wonders of Ancient Greece*. Minneapolis, MN: Twenty-First Century Books, 2008.

Websites

BBC History: Ancient History
http://www.bbc.co.uk/history/ancient/greeks
The "Athens and Democracy" link offers access to a critique of democratic Athens and other information.

The British Museum: Ancient Greece
http://www.ancientgreece.co.uk
Click the "Knowledge & Learning" link to learn more about Greece's great thinkers.

Discovery News: Ancient Greece
http://news.discovery.com/history/tags/ancient-greece.htm
Keep up with the latest news about ancient Greece, such as new discoveries and recent scholarly debates.

History: Ancient Greece
http://www.history.com/topics/ancient-history/ancient-greece
This site briefly outlines the history of ancient Greece and includes links to interesting videos about this ancient culture.

The Met: Ancient Greece, 1000 BC–1 AD
http://www.metmuseum.org/toah/ht/04/eusb.html
A timeline on this website includes an overview of key events with links to more information, including essays on Greek theater, Greek architects, and more.

Index

Page numbers in **boldface** are illustrations. Entries in **boldface** are glossary terms.